World Faiths Today Series
Exploring Hinduism

Who are your friends? Do you know everything about them? Do they know everything about you?

Well, this is a story about friends who do not know everything about one another. But they are starting to learn some things their friends do and why they do them. Read their story and you might learn something new too!

1 Visiting a mandir

Rees and Sara were standing outside a large, red brick building. From the outside, it did not look much different from any other red brick building but Rees and Sara knew that something important was about to happen inside. They watched the growing streams of people walk past them into the building. Rees and Sara searched eagerly among the faces for their friends from school, Rajeev and Meena.

Rajeev and Meena are Hindus. Today, they had promised to take Rees and Sara to a puja service at their Hindu Temple which they call a mandir.

'We are glad that you could make it!' said an excited voice behind Rees and Sara. They swung around and greeted their friends, Rajeev and Meena.

'This mandir is a special place for us,' said Rajeev. 'Look on the wall! Can you see the sacred symbol OM written in Sanskrit? You will find OM inside the building too. It is a symbol of God, who is the Supreme Reality. The mandir is a place where Hindus can come to worship God. It is also a good place to meet other Hindus who live locally.'

When they entered the building, the children removed their shoes and placed them on a shoe rack. After that, they washed their hands.

Rajeev and Meena led Rees and Sara to a large room. Rees and Sara gasped in amazement at what they saw. They were surrounded by colourful shrines with statues and pictures on them. Each shrine had been lovingly decorated with tinsel, lights, and baubles. Placed on the shrines were offerings of food and money.

Rajeev and Meena introduced Rees and Sara to some of the statues and pictures on the shrines.

'These are images of our gods and goddesses,' explained Meena. 'Here is the god Ganesh and the god Shiva. Over there, we have the goddess Durga and the goddess Lakshmi. All the images have been blessed, so we believe that God is present in them.'

'I am confused,' admitted Rees, looking at the gods and goddesses in bewilderment. 'You said that you worshipped God who is the Supreme Reality. Now you say that you have many different gods and goddesses.'

Meena smiled and said, 'A lot of people find it difficult to understand what Hindus mean when they talk about God. A passage from our scriptures says that God is one, though wise men call God by many names. Hindus believe that God, who is the Supreme Reality, can be worshipped in many different forms. You can see some of these forms in the gods and goddesses around you, but there are many more. Hindus often choose to focus on one or more of these forms in their worship.'

The priest rang a bell to announce that the puja service was about to begin. They turned to face the main shrine and listened to the priest reciting a prayer in a language that Rees and Sara did not understand.

The priest offered to God incense, flowers, fruit, nuts, and water. He lit an arti lamp which had five flickering flames, and offered fire to God. After waving the flames over the main shrine, the priest did the same to each of the other shrines in turn. By this time, everyone was singing enthusiastically, and some people were playing the cymbal, drum, and tambourine.

'When we make puja offerings and sing, we show our love and devotion to God,' explained Rajeev.

After the priest had finished visiting all the shrines with the arti lamp, he offered fire to each person in turn. Rees and Sara watched Rajeev and Meena stretch their hands out over the flames and then lightly touch their faces and hair.

At the end of the service the fruit and nuts which had been offered to God were divided out among everyone. This food is called prashad.

'When we accept fire and food which have been offered to God, we receive God's love and blessings,' explained Meena.

Rees and Sara felt that they knew Rajeev and Meena a little better after their visit to the mandir. They had learnt that many Hindus worship God, who is the Supreme Reality, but God can be worshipped in many different forms. In a puja service Hindus show their love and devotion to God and they receive God's love and blessings.

2 Celebrating Diwali

Rees and Sara had been looking forward to this day for weeks. The five-day Hindu festival of Diwali had begun and their friends, Rajeev and Meena, wanted them to share in the celebrations.

Rajeev and Meena's grandmother took them to a special shrine in the local Hindu Temple.

'There is a Diwali story about the characters on this shrine,' she said. 'It is a story of good conquering evil and light banishing darkness. It is about honour, loyalty, and love.'

A long time ago, an old, good king ruled the Indian kingdom of Ayodhara. The king asked his eldest son, Rama, to rule in his place. This pleased everyone apart from one of the king's wives. She wanted her son, Bharata, to rule, not Rama. Cunningly, she reminded the king that he had promised her two wishes.

'My first wish is for my son, Bharata, to become king,' she said. 'My second wish is for Rama to be exiled to the forest for fourteen years.'

Reluctantly, the king agreed. He could not break a promise. So, Rama was exiled to the forest. His beautiful wife Sita and his brother Laksmana insisted on going with him. When the old king died, Bharata asked Rama to return as king but Rama refused because fourteen years had not yet passed. So, Bharata placed Rama's sandals on the throne and promised to look after the kingdom until Rama returned.

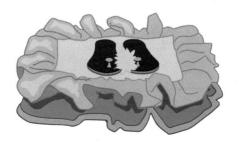

The forest was a dangerous place. The ten-armed and ten-headed evil demon, Ravana, wanted to make Sita his wife. One day Ravana tricked Rama and Laksmana into leaving Sita alone. He then kidnapped Sita and took her to his palace. Even as a prisoner in the palace, Sita refused to marry Ravana.

Rama and Laksmana were heartbroken, and searched for her everywhere. Hanuman, king of the monkeys, helped them. The monkeys discovered that Sita had been taken to the island of Lanka and they fought a ten-day battle to rescue her. Rama killed Ravana with a special bow and arrow.

Triumphantly, Rama, Sita, and Laksmana journeyed back to the kingdom of Ayodhara. The people of Ayodhara lit burning lamps to guide them safely back home. Bharata organised a huge celebration, and welcomed Rama home as the rightful king.

'Diwali means a cluster of lights,' said grandmother. 'During Diwali, we light divas and fill our homes and buildings with light. There are firework displays which remind us of the weapons used to destroy evil in ancient battles. Diwali celebrates the victory of good over evil.'

Back at Rajeev and Meena's house, Rees and Sara admired a colourful pattern in the garden by the front door.

'This is our rangoli pattern for Diwali,' said Meena proudly. 'We spent ages making it. Rangoli patterns are made using flour, rice grains, or coloured chalk.'

'It is very clever,' said Sara. 'I hope that it does not rain because it will be spoiled.'

Rajeev shrugged and said, 'It is not supposed to last forever. It is there to welcome visitors and also the goddess Lakshmi who visits each house during Diwali.'

Inside Rajeev and Meena's house, Rees and Sara noticed that there was a strong smell of paint in the air. They also noticed that everywhere was looking extremely clean and tidy.

'We have helped our parents to clean and paint the house,' said Meena. 'The goddess Lakshmi likes clean and tidy houses. We hope that Lakshmi will give our family good fortune and wealth in the new year ahead.'

Rajeev fetched a picture of Lakshmi and showed the picture to them. Sara thought that Lakshmi looked beautiful and kind. Rees was impressed by the white elephant beside Lakshmi and the coins pouring from Lakshmi's outstretched hand.

Rajeev and Meena's mother helped the children make Indian sweets for Diwali. Some of the sweets were put into boxes to give as presents and the rest were eaten. Later, Rajeev and Meena's relatives arrived to share in a special Diwali meal. Rees and Sara watched the whole family exchange cards and presents.

'Diwali is a time for families to get together,' said Rajeev. 'We try to forget about any arguments or problems and we try to be happy.'

Rees and Sara enjoyed celebrating Diwali with their friends, Rajeev and Meena. They understood that Diwali celebrates the victory of good over evil. Diwali also marks the beginning of the Hindu New Year. So, many Hindus hope that the goddess Lakshmi will bless their homes with good fortune for the coming year. Diwali is a happy time when families can enjoy being together.

3 Some special books

It was World Book Day and Rees's class and Sara's class at school had come together to share some of their favourite books.

Sara's favourite book was a large encyclopaedia for children.

'This encyclopaedia is special to me because it explains how things work,' said Sara. 'If I want to know how electricity works, or why lava comes out of volcanoes, or any other question, I know that I can find the answer in this book.'

Rees's favourite book at that time was a story book that he had just finished reading.

'I enjoyed reading this story because lots of exciting things happen in it,' said Rees. 'The main character in the book is a boy who finds an old map in his grandmother's attic. The map takes the boy on lots of adventures which reveal some dark secrets about one of the families in the village. I think that I will read this story again and again!'

Someone else showed everyone a paper aeroplane construction book, and another pupil had brought an atlas with maps of the world in it.

When it was Rajeev and Meena's turn, they showed the class a book called the Bhagavad Gita.

'The Bhagavad Gita is a special book for many Hindus like us,' said Rajeev. 'The Bhagavad Gita teaches about God's love for us and about how we can love and serve God.'

Later that day, Rees and Sara were walking home from school with Rajeev and Meena.

'Tell us more about your special book, the Bhagavad Gita,' said Sara. 'What sort of book is it?'

'The book is a long poem about a conversation between an archer called Arjuna and Krishna, his charioteer,' replied Meena. Meena explained to Rees and Sara what the conversation was about.

Arjuna did not want to go into battle at the start of a great war because he was afraid of fighting and killing his cousins. This would have been very wrong. But, Krishna argued that a warrior had a duty to fight for justice and that Arjuna would be committing a greater wrong if he did not fight.

Krishna then revealed his true identity to Arjuna. Krishna is the Lord of the Universe, the Supreme Reality, and God who had taken on human form.

Krishna taught Arjuna three important lessons. The first lesson was that everyone has duties and that they must do them. Warriors have duties, parents have duties, and teachers have duties. All of us have duties.

The second lesson was that people should not expect rewards for the things that they do. They should do things because they are the right things to do and because they love God.

The third lesson was that people's efforts and energy should focus on worshipping God through love and devotion.

Understanding these three lessons leads to true happiness.

'These teachings are still very important for many Hindus today,' said Meena.

'Did Arjuna go into battle?' asked Rees, eager to hear the end of the story.

'Yes,' replied Meena. 'Arjuna did go to battle. He had understood Krishna's three lessons.'

Hindus have many other special books as well as the Bhagavad Gita,' said Rajeev. 'Some of my favourites are the great Hindu myths about the gods and goddesses. If you come to Meena's dance lesson, you can find out more about these.'

At Meena's dance lesson Rees and Sara watched a type of dance that they had never seen before. Meena and the other dancers used their faces, necks, and hands as well as the rest of their bodies when they danced to the music.

'This form of dancing comes from South India,' said Rajeev. 'Through dance and mime, the dancers retell the great Hindu myths. This type of dancing is very ancient. It is found in a book on dance and drama which existed around two thousand years ago.'

Rajeev explained that the dancers want to do more than simply entertain people and retell Hindu stories. Through dancing, they show their love and devotion to God. This means that they worship God when they dance.

Rees and Sara had learnt some new things about their friends, Rajeev and Meena. They now knew that Hindus have many special books, but for Rajeev and Meena's family the Bhagavad Gita is particularly special. The Bhagavad Gita teaches about the meaning of duty and the way to worship God through love and devotion. Rees and Sara had learnt also that many Hindus enjoy the great Hindu myths about the gods and the goddesses. Dancing these stories is yet another way of worshipping God.

4 Caring for others and the world

Rees and Sara were riding their bikes in the street with their friends Rajeev and Meena. The sound of shrieking and laughter caught their attention and they went to discover what the fuss was about. In a nearby garden, Rees and Sara's six-year-old neighbour, Billy, was crouching over something with a gang of his friends.

'Squash it! It is going to get away,' one child ordered, prodding at the thing with a stick.

'Keep it away from me!' another screamed, jumping up and down.

Rajeev got off his bike and walked over to the younger children.

'What is going on here?' he asked, sternly.

The children immediately fell back, revealing what they had been doing. Billy and his friends had rolled back a stone and found a huge black beetle under it. The beetle was now desperately trying to escape death by scurrying for cover.

'It is only a beetle,' replied Billy, sulkily. 'It has got away now.'

'Good,' said Rajeev. 'It is very wrong to hurt or kill any living creature, especially if you do it deliberately. You could have been born a beetle instead of a human being. Imagine how the beetle felt. A beetle has as much right to life as you have.'

After this, Rajeev explained to Rees and Sara why he had to stop Billy and his friends from killing the beetle.

'Meena and I are Hindus,' said Rajeev. 'Many Hindus believe that it is wrong to harm or kill living creatures. There are two reasons why we believe this. The first reason is that Hindus believe that every living thing is special. This is because every living thing has a soul inside it. When the body dies, the soul moves into a new body. This happens again and again and again. Everyone goes through many bodies, and not just human bodies! This means that many Hindus respect all forms of life.'

'So, a beetle is never just a beetle,' said Rees thoughtfully.

'Exactly,' said Rajeev. 'The second reason is that Hindus believe that God created the universe and everything in it. Everything has rules to follow so that the world works properly. A river has to flow to the sea, the sun has to give light and heat to the Earth, a plant has to grow and provide food for other creatures. Everything follows its own rules, and if it does not, there is chaos.'

Meena nodded her head vigorously.

'Human beings can cause chaos,' she said. 'This is because human beings are intelligent enough to choose whether to follow the rules or not.'

Rajeev gently rolled the stone back and said, 'Billy and his friends were in danger of breaking the important rule of respecting animal life. That is why I stopped them killing the beetle.'

Billy and his friends are just little kids,' said Meena. 'When adults break the rules, it is a lot more serious. There is a true story about some people called the tree huggers which helps to explain why.'

Over thirty years ago, powerful companies were given permission to cut down parts of the forests in the Himalayas. These companies made a lot of money for themselves from selling the timber. They did not think about the problems that they were causing in the area. The local people relied on the trees for food and fuel, and this was being threatened. The trees were important for the environment, and this was being damaged.

In 1973 a group of local women agreed that they had to do something to stop the damage. They decided that they would not violently destroy anything, like the timber companies were doing. Instead, they would make a peaceful protest.

The women put their arms around the threatened trees, hugging them. The companies would have to cut the women down first before they could get to the trees! The women were successful and the tree cutting stopped. After this, many other ordinary Indians have done the same thing to save their livelihoods and the environment.

Rees and Sara felt that they knew a little more about their friends, Rajeev and Meena. They understood that many Hindus believe that it is wrong to hurt or kill other living creatures. All living things possess a soul and all living things have duties to fulfil. Human beings have a duty to look after others and the environment. A great deal of pain and suffering is caused when people forget this and think only about their own needs.

5 Food

Rees and Sara were sitting around a large, circular table feeling very hungry. They had been invited to share a special meal with their friends, Rajeev and Meena and their family.

Rajeev and Meena's mother had prepared a selection of Indian dishes for Rees and Sara to try. In the centre of the table stood an assortment of rice and vegetable dishes as well as naan and chapatti breads. Everyone helped themselves to the food.

'Our religion, Hinduism, comes from India originally although today Hindus live all over the world,' explained Meena. 'These are some of our family's favourite Indian dishes. Like many Hindus, we are vegetarians because we believe that it is wrong to kill animals for food. None of the food on this table contains meat.'

Rees and Sara were surprised that simple vegetables and rice could taste so interesting. For them, vegetables were usually eaten with a main meat or fish dish. Vegetables were rarely eaten on their own.

'We use many different spices in our food which gives it the interesting flavours,' explained Rajeev and Meena's mother. She showed Rees and Sara unfamiliar ingredients like garam masala, ginger, cumin, fenugreek seeds, mustard seeds, coriander seeds, chillies, peppers, and turmeric.

'Not all Hindus are vegetarian like we are, but most Hindus will refuse to harm or kill cows and eat their meat,' said Rajeev. 'This is because Hindus believe that cows are very special animals. Traditionally, in India, cows have been important for farming, food, and transport. Cows give milk and all the other things which come from milk. Bulls plough fields and pull carts. Hindus believe that it is wrong to harm an animal which gives us so much. In some states in India killing cows has been made illegal!'

Rajeev and Meena's father pointed out that cows were special in Hinduism for religious reasons too. He showed Rees and Sara a lamp by a small shrine where their family worshipped God every morning.

'The arti lamp is lit as part of our worship,' he said. 'The lamp burns with ghee instead of wax. Ghee is clarified butter. This is made from cows' milk.'

Rajeev and Meena's father then showed Rees and Sara a picture of Krishna and Radha.

'This is God in the human form of Krishna,' he explained. 'When we think of Krishna, we often think of cows. Krishna rides a white calf and beside him stands his favourite cowherd girl, Radha. Radha loves and devotes herself to Krishna completely and Krishna loves Radha. Together, they symbolise the perfect relationship between God and a human being.'

After supper, the four children played a board game for a while. They had to answer general knowledge questions and Meena was winning.

'I feel a lot better after eating,' said Meena, contentedly. 'I can concentrate better. I think that I might even win this game.'

Rajeev paused, thought, and remembered something.

'Many Hindus believe that the type of food we eat has an effect on our bodies and minds,' he said. 'Some foods make us feel dull, sluggish, and without energy. Some foods make us feel excited and full of action. Other foods make us feel happy and healthy as well as giving us a long life. A lot of the vegetarian food that we ate tonight is considered to be the best diet by many Hindus.'

That evening Rees and Sara had learnt a great deal about their friends, Rajeev and Meena. They now knew that for many Hindus eating means more than simply filling the stomach and staying alive. Often Hindus are vegetarian because they believe that it is wrong to kill animals for food. They also believe that what people eat affects the way people feel and think as well as their health. Cows are particularly special for Hindus because they are so useful and they are also connected to Krishna.

On their way home, Rees and Sara felt that they would like to share some of their own special things with Rajeev and Meena. Now, what would they choose first?

In the World Faiths Today Series Rees and Sara learn about the major world faiths in their own country. The seven stories in the series are:

- Exploring Islam
- Exploring Judaism
- Exploring the Parish Church
- Exploring the Orthodox Church
- Exploring Hinduism
- Exploring Buddhism
- Exploring Sikhism

Welsh National Centre for Religious Education
Bangor University
Bangor
Gwynedd
Wales

First published 2008.

Sponsored by the Welsh Assembly Government.

British Library Cataloguing-in-Publication Data
A catalogue record for this book is available from the British Library.

ISBN 978-1-85357-190-9

Printed and bound in Wales by Gwasg Dwyfor.